IMAGES
of America

JAMAICA PLAIN

James Michael Curley said in his book *I'd Do It Again* that "I always had a local Chinese constituency, who gave me this costume, in which I posed for them in my library." The Curley House, with its shamrock cut-out shutters, was built at 350 The Jamaicaway in 1915 by Boston architect Joseph McGinnis and has been designated a Boston landmark. (Courtesy of Jamaica Plain Branch of the Boston Public Library, hereinafter referred to as the BPL.)

IMAGES
of America

JAMAICA PLAIN

Anthony Mitchell Sammarco

ARCADIA

First printed in 1997.
Reprinted in 1999, 2000, 2001.

Published by Arcadia Publishing,
an imprint of Tempus Publishing, Inc.
2A Cumberland Street
Charleston, SC 29401

Printed in Great Britain.

For all general information contact Arcadia Publishing at:
Telephone 843-853-2070
Fax 843-853-0044
E-Mail sales@arcadiapublishing.com

For customer service and orders:
Toll-Free 1-888-313-2665

Visit us on the internet at http://www.arcadiapublishing.com

Students in a cooking class at the Bowditch School in 1893 pose around their preparation
stations, with muslin mop caps and protective aprons over their dresses.

Contents

Introduction   7

1.   Early Jamaica Plain   9

2.   The Great Estates   23

3.   Places of Worship   35

4.   Schools   49

5.   Arnold Arboretum and Forest Hills Cemetery   67

6.   Jamaica Pond   77

7.   A Medley of Community Services   87

8.   A Streetcar Suburb   107

9.   Forest Hills   115

10.   Modes of Transportation   121

Acknowledgments   128

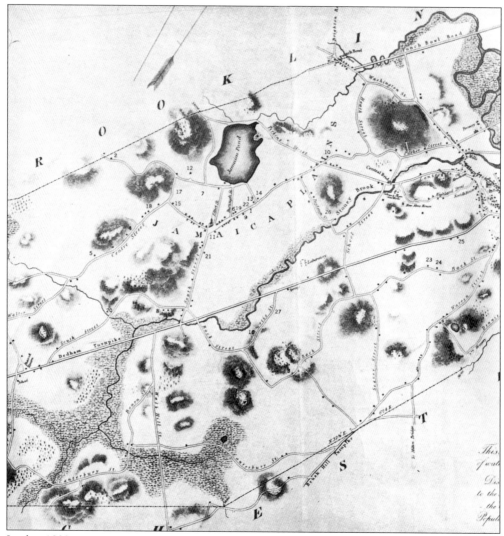

In this 1832 map, "Jamaica Plains" is the area surrounding Jamaica Pond. The Stoney (Stony) Brook was later filled in. The area is shown with most of the residents living along Centre and South Streets, and the rest of the town is a sparsely settled section of Roxbury, Massachusetts. (Courtesy of the Boston Public Library, hereinafter referred to as the BPL.)

Introduction

Jamaica Plain is today a neighborhood of Boston, but prior to the mid-nineteenth century, it was a part of Roxbury, Massachusetts, and was often referred to as the "Jamaica End" or "Pond Plain" area of the town. The issue of the naming of Jamaica Plain is a somewhat ambiguous one, but many credit the derivation to the fact that merchants who lived in the town "made their money in Jamaica Rum" and consequently had something to do with the name. Asked how they preferred their rum, the merchants are reputed to have replied "Jamaica, *plain*." That makes for a good story, but the most probable reason the area was named Jamaica Plain was the fact that Oliver Cromwell had seized the island of Jamaica from the Spaniards in 1655 and that "its rum, sugar, and other products had already found their way to the adjacent port of Boston." Further, the flatness of the land surrounding the pond was referred to as a plain, and the name had evolved by the late 1660s as recorded in the Minutes of the Roxbury Town Records, which states that Hugh Thomas conveyed property for the benefit of a school for "the people at the Jamaica end of the town of Roxbury."

One traveled man who knew this country well in the early nineteenth century said that "Jamaica Plain is the Eden of America." However, regardless of how its name evolved, Jamaica Plain "is one of the loveliest spots in New England. It abounds in springs and brooks, and its soil, light and gravelly, is easily cultivated." The area remained primarily farmland for the first two centuries after Massachusetts Bay was settled by the Puritans in 1630, but by the early nineteenth century, Jamaica Plain was an attractive area where "elegant country seats are delightfully situated on the banks of the lake and elsewhere, and the Plain is dotted with the tasteful cottages of business men, who retire every evening from their avocations in the city to this charming spot."

Reverend John Eliot, pastor of the Roxbury Meeting House, had bequeathed a 75-acre tract of land in 1689 that was to support the school in the area. Now known as the Eliot School on Eliot Street, the bequest stipulated that the school open its doors to all children, white, black, and Native American.

Incorporated in 1804, today the school offers such courses as sewing, woodworking, upholstery, and gold leafing for all, regardless of their background, in compliance to Eliot's bequest.

By the nineteenth century, Jamaica Plain was no longer a country town with wealthy summer residents, such as Governors Sir Francis Bernard and John Hancock, who kept summer houses near Jamaica Pond, but was a greatly changed area. In 1826, the first hourly omnibuses ran from Jamaica Plain to Boston, at a fare of 25¢. The Boston and Providence Railroad line was put through Jamaica Plain in 1834 and spurred the development of the farms and estates. An early development was Glenvale Park, the area laid out in 1848 as Chestnut and Lamartine Streets. William Hyslop Sumner, whose estate was on Sumner Hill, developed the former Greenough estate in the 1850s, with new streets such as Carolina and Greenough Avenues, and Elm,

Roanoke, Revere, and Sedgwick Streets. Sumner was the son of Governor Increase Sumner and was the developer in 1833 of East Boston, which was inherited through his mother and acquired the remaining portion from relatives. As a land developer, he was without peer, and his own mansion was on the crest of Roanoke Street, within sight of the railroad tracks, a location that at that time connoted progress, not blight. The railroad had depots, which are perpetuated by the present Stony Brook and Green Street Stations on the Orange Line located on the same sites as the original depots. After the Civil War, horse-drawn streetcars were extended along Washington and Centre Streets, and this transportation led to the influx of new residents who were instrumental in the development of Jamaica Plain as a "Streetcar Suburb" of Boston.

After West Roxbury, which included the present neighborhoods of West Roxbury, Roslindale, and Jamaica Plain, separated from the City of Roxbury in 1851, the area of Centre and South Streets became the new town's center. West Roxbury Town Hall, later known as Curtis Hall, was built in 1868 as the center of town government. In 1871, on a triangular park opposite the town hall at the junction of Centre and South Streets, the original site of the Eliot School of 1676, which is often referred to as Monument Square, the town of West Roxbury erected a granite monument. The monument, designed by W.W. Lummus, was dedicated to the memory of their townsmen who gave the ultimate sacrifice during the Civil War.

Though the town encouraged development, the rural aspect of Jamaica Plain was protected by the bequest of Benjamin Bussey for an agricultural experimentation station on his former estate. After James Arnold of New Bedford bequeathed a legacy to Harvard College, the Bussey farm became known as the Arnold Arboretum, a 265-acre tract that is still considered one of the greatest gardens in the world. The Bussey Institute opened in 1871, and specimen plants from around the world were cultivated here prior to being planted in the arboretum. Arnold Arboretum, literally a jewel of a park, was laid out by Frederick Law Olmstead and is still a vital link in what has been termed Boston's "Emerald Necklace." The establishment of Forest Hills Cemetery in 1848 by the city of Roxbury led to an arboretum cemetery that was the inspiration of Henry A.S. Dearborn, a former mayor of Roxbury and president of the Massachusetts Horticultural Society. Dearborn, who had been instrumental in the laying out of Mount Auburn Cemetery, created a picturesque "rural cemetery" where nature and art combined to create not just a place to bury the dead, but a place where they could be mourned with a sense of serenity and reflective contemplation.

Today, Jamaica Plain is a neighborhood of wide appeal, not only for its close proximity to Boston but its many suburban aspects. It has been home to five mayors of Boston: James Michael Curley, Andrew J. Peters, Malcom Nichols, Maurice Tobin, and John Collins. The open spaces of Jamaica Pond, Stony Brook, and Forest Hills Cemetery, as well as the Arnold Arboretum, perpetuate the concept of the "Eden of America," but they also offer activities such as walking, boating, and hiking for city dwellers. Though Jamaica Plain has been a neighborhood of the City of Boston since 1874, it has continued to offer the same amenities that attracted "Streetcar Suburb" residents over a century ago.

One
Early Jamaica Plain

The Third Parish in Roxbury was established in 1769 through the generosity of Benjamin and Suzanna Pemberton. Built at the junction of Centre and South Streets, on land bequeathed to the town by the Apostle Eliot, the old meetinghouse also had a bell donated in 1783 by Governor John Hancock, that had recently been taken from the New Brick Church in Boston. The parsonage is seen on the left, directly behind the meetinghouse. (Courtesy of the BPL.)

The Curtis House was built in 1639 at what is now the corner of Lamartine and Paul Gore Streets by William Curtis, whose wife Sarah was the sister of Reverend John Eliot. The house was photographed about 1880, with a group of people standing in front of the ancient landmark. The house, which was continuously occupied by the Curtis family for eight generations, was demolished in 1887. (Courtesy of the BPL.)

The Samuel Curtis House was built in 1722 on Centre Street and on a tract of land bound by Boylston, Curtis, and Sheridan Streets. The house was photographed in 1910, when it was offered for sale, being publicized as "the oldest house in Jamaica Plain occupying its original site." Unfortunately, the house was demolished and the land later developed.

10

The May House was built by John Bridge about 1650 on May Street near the Arborway, and the home was set back from the street with a drive bordered by low-clipped hedges. Ebenezer May, a founder of the Third Parish in Jamaica Plain, and his son Lemuel lived in the house that was set on almost 30 acres with numerous fruit trees.

The Hallowell House was built in 1738 at the corner of Centre and Boylston Streets and was the home of Benjamin Hallowell, a Loyalist who left Boston in 1776. Though confiscated by the state after the Revolution, the estate was claimed in 1801 by Ward Nicholas Hallowell (1749–1828), who later changed his name to Ward Nicholas Boylston. He was a generous man, and his "liberality was commemorated by a school, a market and a street" in Boston. The house was demolished about 1924.

The Loring-Greenough House was built in 1760 for Joshua Loring, a British Naval officer and a Loyalist who left Boston in 1776. During the Revolution, the house was used as a hospital for the Colonials. The house was later purchased by Ann Doane, who married David S. Greenough, and their descendants lived here until 1924. The estate was once quite extensive. Today, this house is on the National Register of Historic Places and is maintained by the Jamaica Plain Tuesday Club. (Courtesy of the BPL.)

A walkway leading to a side entrance of the Loring-Greenough House is flanked with beds of Japanese irises. (Courtesy of the BPL.)

Linden Hall was built in 1755 at the corner of Centre and Pond Streets by John Gould for his son-in-law, Reverend John Troutbeck. Troutbeck was assistant rector at King's Chapel in Boston and "a celebrated distiller." Named for the linden trees that once lined the walkway to the house, Linden Hall was later used as a preparatory academy by Charles W. Greene. (Courtesy of the BPL.)

The open land and country setting in Jamaica Plain attracted residents, such as Stephen M. Allen, who built his house in the mid-1850s at 44 Allandale Street, just off Centre Street. (Courtesy of the BPL.)

The "Boston & Jamaica Plains" omnibus was sketched in 1861 by Mr. Champney for Ballou's *Drawing Room Companion* as the vehicle made its way along Winter Street in Boston during a snowstorm. (Courtesy of the BPL.)

JAMAICA PLAIN OMNIBUSES.

NEW ARRANGEMENT.... APRIL 1, 1853.

The Coaches will leave Jamaica Plain at 6, 7, 8, 9, 10, 11, 12, A. M. and 1, 2, 3, 4 5, 6, 7 and 8, P. M.
Leave Boston at 7, 8, 9, 10, 11, 12, A. M. and 1, 2, 3, 4, 5, 6, 7, 8, 9, P. M.

The Coaches leaving Jamaica Plain at 8 and 10, A. M., and 1 and 4, P. M. will pass round through Eliot and Pond streets and May's Lane BEFORE leaving the Office, while the Coaches leaving Boston at the same hours will pass through the same streets AFTER arriving at the Office.

FARE, 12 1-2 Cents, or 10 Tickets for $1.

SUNDAYS a Coach leaves Jamaica Plain at 9 1-4, A. M. and 2, P. M., and Boston at 12, M. and 5 P. M. FARE, 25 CENTS; SIX TICKETS FOR $1.

OFFICE IN BOSTON, No. 2 MONTGOMERY PLACE.

☞ Private parties can be provided with Omnibuses at any time at short notice. Horses, Carriages, and Saddle Horses to let, at the Stable on Centre street, (formerly the Seaver Stable.) Also, Stabling for Horses.

BURBANK & THOMPSON, Proprietors.

The Jamaica Plain omnibuses connected Boston and Jamaica Plain hourly at a 12½ ¢ fare. The horse-drawn omnibuses were the predecessors of the street railway. (Courtesy of the BPL.)

Centre Street was a quiet thoroughfare in this 1880 photograph. Laid out in 1663 and known as the "Dedham Road," it was renamed in 1825. On the right is the spire of the Old Universalist Church. (Courtesy of the West Roxbury Historical Society.)

Centre Street, seen in this 1885 photograph, was built up with business blocks between Thomas and Green Streets. A mother pushes a perambulator on the right, and the local firehouse can be seen on the left. (Courtesy of the BPL.)

The Allandale Mineral Spring Water Pavilion was opened in 1876 and was a popular destination for those feeling poorly, since its "cures and healing power has placed it in rank with the most celebrated Springs of the world." Two men stand near the counters where the mineral water was offered and quaffed with relish.

The trademark of the Allandale Mineral Springs Water attested to the fact that it could "allay all internal inflammation, while its action is very marked in the cure of Dyspepsia, all Kidney Complaints, Diabetes, Gravel, Canker, Dropsy, Catarrh, Nervousness, Bladder Diseases and Constipation, Eczema and all Skin Diseases." Obviously, a miracle in every sip!

The Soldiers' Monument was dedicated on September 14, 1871, in memory of those from West Roxbury who died in the service of their country during the Rebellion of 1861–1865. Inscribed are the names of the following heroes: Brig. General T.J.C. Amory, Lt. Colonel Lucius M. Sargent Jr., Capt. William B. Williams, Capt. William H. Simpkins, Capt. William F. Cochran, Adjutant Henry Bond, Lt. Charles Russell, Lt. Alfred Glover, Sergeant Charles Manning, Sergeant Charles Brazier, Corporal Levi Lincoln, James Gilson, James Thomas, Charles Stearns, Charles Harper, Joseph Harper, Thomas Baker, Horace Goodwin, John Burke, Munroe George, Curtis Grover, Michael Dolan, and Edward Norton. (Courtesy of the West Roxbury Historical Society.)

The Soldiers' Monument stands on a small triangular park, opposite the First Parish Church at the junction of South and Centre Streets. The stone church was built in 1854 by Boston architect Nathaniel J. Bradlee. In the rear of the church is an eighteenth-century burial ground.

17

Curtis Hall was designed by the architect George Ropes Jr. and was built in 1868 as the West Roxbury Town Hall. The building was donated to the town by Nelson Curtis and was dedicated on October 8, 1868. A fire destroyed the mansard roof in 1908, and the City of Boston commissioned architect Lewis H. Bacon to remodel the hall and add a new roof, which was completed in 1912.

A gymnasium was located on the third floor of Curtis Hall, which was also known as the Jamaica Plain Municipal Building. In this c. 1912 photograph, young ladies exercise with dumbbells; also available were free boxing, dancing instruction, basketball, handball, track, indoor games, and sports of all kinds.

The swimming pool inside the Municipal Building allowed for swimming instruction throughout the year.

Judge John W. McKim was appointed judge of the municipal court for West Roxbury in 1874 by Governor Talbot. He was appointed judge of the probate court for Suffolk County in 1877. (Courtesy of the BPL.)

The police station in Jamaica Plain (District 13) was designed by George Clough, Boston city architect, for a combined police station and municipal court. It was built in 1875 on Seaverns Avenue. Today, the former police station has been remodeled for use as housing. (Courtesy of the BPL.)

Members of the Jamaica Plain police force stand across Seaverns Avenue at the turn of the century, with the police station on the left. (Courtesy of the Jamaica Plain Historical Society.)

Two firemen pose with a horse-drawn chemical engine in this 1880 photograph at the corner of Centre and Burroughs Streets. These engines used chemicals rather than water to fight fires, but were still pulled by horses to the scene of a fire. (Courtesy of the Jamaica Plain Historical Society.)

Firemen pose outside of Engine Company 18 on Centre Street, near Myrtle Street, in 1904 with a three-horse chemical engine "at the ready." (Courtesy of the BPL.)

Photographed in 1885 at the corner of Centre and Burroughs Streets with a "hook and ladder" are John Lynch, driver of Ladder 10, and Mark Davis, the call captain standing on the center of the truck. On the left is the Seaverns House. (Courtesy of the Jamaica Plain Historical Society.)

Posing on a "modern fire engine" outside the fire doors of the Forest Hills Fire Station in 1912 are five members of the Boston Fire Department.

Two
The Great Estates

Lochstead was built by Donald McKay on the banks of Jamaica Pond. It was later sold to David Wallace. Members of the Wallace Family posed for this photograph about 1870. Lochstead Road, which runs from the Jamaicaway to Centre Street, perpetuates the name of the estate. (Courtesy of the BPL.)

The Weld House was a small mansion at 310 South Street, at the corner of Asticou Road, just west of Washington Street at Forest Hills. Built by William Gordon Weld, it later became the home of Andrew J. Peters, mayor of Boston from 1918 to 1921. (Courtesy of the BPL.)

William Gordon Weld (1775–1825) was a merchant who founded a fleet of China-trading vessels and who also imported wines from Spain and Portugal on his ship *Mary*. (Courtesy of the BPL.)

Benjamin Bussey (1757–1842), a silversmith and Revolutionary War veteran, built this house in Jamaica Plain in 1815. After Bussey's death, the estate was purchased by Thomas Lothrop Motley, a president of the Massachusetts Society for Promoting Agriculture and brother of the noted historian John Lothrop Motley. The estate, known as Woodland Hills, had the first Jersey cows imported to this country in 1851. The mansion was later demolished in 1940. (Courtesy of David Rooney.)

"Peter Parley" was the nom de plume of children's author Samuel G. Goodrich (1793–1860), onetime consul of the United States at Paris. Author of 170 books for children, Goodrich was also editor of *The Token*. His estate in Jamaica Plain was later developed for modest houses in the area between Centre and Green Streets and the railroad tracks.

The Wallis House, built by Mordecai Lincoln Wallis, was an impressive Greek Revival mansion on Allandale Street. Members of the Wallis family pose on the side of the carriage drive in 1889. (Courtesy of the Jamaica Plain Historical Society.)

Though many of the great estates were designed by architects, most of the smaller houses in Jamaica Plain were designed and built by local builders. John J. Shaw was a carpenter and builder on Green Street and provided the services of "Building and Jobbing." (Courtesy of the BPL.)

Pinebank (Number 1) was built in 1802 by China trade merchant James Perkins (1761–1822) as a Federal country house on the banks of Jamaica Pond. The estate was named for the great profusion of evergreens that dotted the property.

Pinebank (Number 2) was built in 1848 on the site of the original house by Edward Newton Perkins. Designed by the French architect Lemoulnier, it burned two decades later. In a steep descent to the pond, Perkins installed the freestone staircase from the Hancock Mansion on Beacon Hill that had been demolished in 1863.

William Hyslop Sumner (1780–1861) was married to Maria Foster Greenough (1793–1843), the widow of David Stoddard Greenough. Maria inherited the estate that was later developed by William. Sumner was the son of Governor Increase Sumner and the developer of East Boston, Massachusetts. He later left land for the building of Saint John's Church, of which he was senior warden at the time of his death.

The Sumner House was built at 6 Roanoke Avenue at the crest of "Sumner Hill," a development of the Greenough Estate by William H. Sumner. The Sumner's neighbor was Reverend Charles Dole, whose son was James Drummond Dole (1877–1958), who had studied at the Bussey Institute. In 1901, James founded the Dole Pineapple Company on the Sandwich Islands. (Courtesy of the BPL.)

The Parkman House, seen from the rear in 1894, was on the banks of Jamaica Pond. The house was later demolished. The Parkman Memorial, designed by Daniel Chester French, was erected in 1906 on the former site of the house between Prince Street and Parkman Drive. On the base of the monument is written: "Here where for many years he lived and where he died friends of Francis Parkman have placed this seat in token of their admiration for his character and for his achievements." (Courtesy of the BPL.)

Francis Parkman (1823–1893) was a noted historian and writer whose house on the banks of Jamaica Pond served him as a refuge. He was also a professor of horticulture in the agricultural school at Harvard between 1871 and 1872, and at his garden in Jamaica Plain, he hybridized the *Lilium Parkmanni*, a speckled red lily.

Seen here about 1880, the dock by the Parkman House was a wood projection on the bank of Jamaica Pond where small boats could be docked. The rear piazza of the Parkman House can be seen on the left. (Courtesy of the BPL.)

Lakeville Manor was a gracious brick mansion that was built in 1797 on Centre Street, near Lakeville Road. Built as the home of Charles Beaumont, it was later the residence of Mr. Du Ballet. Horatio Greenough, the noted sculptor, lived here in the mid-nineteenth century and is reputed to have carved *The Chanting Cherubs* while living here. (Courtesy of the BPL.)

Lochstead was a fanciful Gothic Revival cottage on the banks of Jamaica Pond that adjoined the Parkman property. A rowboat is on the right, near the boathouse of the Wallace Family. (Courtesy of the BPL.)

The William P. Gould Estate was at the corner of Perkins and Centre Streets. (Courtesy of the Jamaica Plain Historical Society.)

Senator Gaspar Bacon lived in this rambling mansion at 222 Prince Street, which overlooked Jamaica Pond. (Courtesy of the West Roxbury Historical Society.)

Nutwood was the home of Charles Moorefield Storey, a prominent attorney, and it was a large Stick Style mansion at 229 Perkins Street, on the banks of Jamaica Pond. (Courtesy of the BPL.)

Friends enjoy a coaching party in Jamaica Plain in the 1890s. With an old coach draped in fabric and bedecked with a profusion of flowers, friends pose for the photographer as a young boy holds a banner saying, "Jamaica Plain." (Courtesy of the West Roxbury Historical Society.)

Arriving at their destination, members of the coaching party pose for a group photograph. These parties were all the rage at the turn of the century. (Courtesy of the West Roxbury Historical Society.)

Members of the Perkins family sit on the entrance porch to Pinebank (Number 3), which was built in 1870 for Edward Newton Perkins. Designed by the Boston architectural firm of Sturgis and Brigham, the lavish use of terra cotta and ornamental brick made for an impressive country house. Used by the family until 1892, when the estate was purchased by the Boston Park Commission, today it stands forlornly abandoned, awaiting restoration. (Courtesy of the BPL.)

The Curtis Farm had a "Hoeing Surprise Party" on June 4, 1873. Men, complete with their own hoes, stand in the rear of the Curtis House, with three fashionably dressed girls and a small brass band on the far right before setting out for their field work. (Courtesy of Martha Tyer Curtis and the late Nelson Curtis Jr.)

Three
Places of Worship

Parishioners leave Saint Thomas Aquinas Church after Sunday mass during World War II. Built in 1873 at the corner of South and Saint Joseph Streets, Saint Thomas Aquinas Church was designed by the noted architect Patrick J. Keeley. On the right of the front entrance is a billboard listing parishioners serving in the armed forces during the war. (Courtesy of the Jamaica Plain Historical Society.)

Reverend William Gordon, D.D., (1730–1807) was the first pastor of the Third Religious Society in Roxbury, or what was later known as the Jamaica Plain Unitarian Church, from 1772 to 1786. (Courtesy of the Jamaica Plain Historical Society.)

The Jamaica Plain Unitarian Church was built in 1854 of stone and granite and was designed by Boston architect Nathaniel J. Bradlee. A streetcar approaches from Centre Street on the right, and the Soldiers' Monument graces the triangular park in the foreground.

Saint John's Church was a small wooden chapel built in 1841 in the center of Saint John Street, set back from Centre Street, and was the first Episcopal church in Jamaica Plain. (Courtesy of the BPL.)

Reverend Mark Anthony De Wolf Howe, D.D., was the rector of Saint James Church in Roxbury and minister in charge of Saint John's Church in Jamaica Plain from 1832 to 1841. Reverend Howe maintained a life-long interest in the church, and in 1885, he preached the sermon at the consecration of the present church on Roanoke Avenue. (Courtesy of the BPL.)

Saint John's Episcopal Church was built in 1882 on land donated by William Hyslop Sumner, whose estate was adjacent to the church site. Designed by Harris M. Stephenson (1845–1909), it was consecrated in 1885 and is still an impressive stone church on an elevated knoll on Sumner Hill.

The men and boys' choir of Saint John's Church pose for a picture in this c. 1900 photograph.

The rector, wardens, and vestry of Saint John's Church pose on the church steps in 1941 during the centenary observances of the founding of the church. From left to right are: (front row) Vincent Hazard, Dr. M. Victor Safford, Fred Kraut, Dr. Willis Hazard, and Charles Godfrey; (middle row) James Schlopp, Griswold Tyng, Robert Schlopp, and Sewell Brackett; (back row) Harry Lees, John Wilson, Edward Goodearl, Carl Mittell, Reverend Thomas Campbell, and John Cook. (Courtesy of the BPL.)

In 1935, the present Georgian Revival-style Central Congregational Church was built at 85 Seaverns Avenue. (Courtesy of the West Roxbury Historical Society.)

The second edifice of the Central Congregational Church was built in 1872, at the corner of Elm Street and Seaverns Avenue. An impressive Romanesque Revival church, it had a soaring tower with a steeple clock visible from the hill. (Courtesy of the BPL.)

Reverend Alonzo H. Quint, D.D., was the first pastor of the Central Congregational Church, serving from 1853 to 1863. (Courtesy of the BPL.)

BOYLSTON CONGREGATIONAL
CHURCH, JAMAICA PLAIN

The Boylston Congregational Church is
a Shingle Style church at the corner of
Boylston and Amory Streets.

The Upham Memorial Methodist
Episcopal Church was at the corner of
Wachusett and Patten Streets in Forest
Hills. (Courtesy of the West Roxbury
Historical Society.)

The Covenant Congregational Church was built in 1935 and is located at 455 Morton Street, adjacent to the West Roxbury Court House, which was built in 1922. (Courtesy of the West Roxbury Historical Society.)

Saint Andrew Ukranian Orthodox Church was built in 1958 on Orchardhill Road in Forest Hills. The onion-shaped domes of the church add a distinctly Slavic feeling to the hill.

The original facade of Saint Thomas Aquinas Church looked somewhat different from today when it was completed in 1873. Patrick Keeley, was a noted architect who designed the Cathedral of the Holy Cross in Boston, as well as numerous other Catholic churches in Boston. (Courtesy of the BPL.)

Parishioners of Saint Thomas Aquinas Church often sent their children to the parish school, Saint Leo XIII, rather than the public schools in Jamaica Plain. The parish school was built in 1890 on Jamaica Street. Here, a priest stands to the right of the parochial school students at the turn of the century. (Courtesy of the BPL.)

Parishioners of Saint Thomas Aquinas Church walk home after Sunday mass in the late 1930s. The twin spires and the facade had been rebuilt from the original design. (Courtesy of the West Roxbury Historical Society.)

An early group of thespians at Saint Thomas Aquinas Church pose for a group photograph in the 1930s. (Courtesy of the BPL.)

The original Saint Leo XIII School was quite a building. It had three stories, with four classrooms on the first and second floors and an assembly hall on the third floor. A bell was donated by Pope Leo XIII and hung in the belfry surmounting the roof. (Courtesy of the BPL.)

The Saint Thomas Aquinas Prep Band was the Catholic Youth Organization Circuit and Festival Champion in 1967. (Courtesy of the BPL.)

Our Lady of Lourdes was originally a mission of Saint Thomas Aquinas Church. Designed by Boston architect Edward T.P. Graham and built in 1931 on Montebello Road, the church is as impressive as it is grand in its Tuscan Romanesque design.

Saint Andrew the Apostle Parish was founded in 1918 and is at 40 Walk Hill Street in Forest Hills. (Courtesy of the BPL.)

The original wooden church of Blessed Sacrament Church was built in 1891 at the corner of Centre and Creighton Streets, near Hyde Square.

The new Blessed Sacrament Church is considered among the most impressive of the churches in the Boston Archdiocese.

This image shows the altar and interior of the Blessed Sacrament Church.

The Monastery of the Sisters of Saint Clare is on Centre Street, just off the Jamaicaway. Dependent on offerings from the public, the nuns make all sorts of embroidery, priests' robes, and spiritual bouquets. In the center of the circular drive is a bronze statue of Saint Francis of Assisi (1182–1237) that was presented in 1937 by Miss Florence Vegkley in memory of Henry and Anne Kenney. (Courtesy of the West Roxbury Historical Society.)

Four

Schools

A group of students participate in a cooking class at the Bowditch School in 1893. Taught by a domestic science instructor how to prepare a wholesome and nutritious dinner, these students could then practice their lessons at home.

The Eliot School was founded in 1676 and endowed in 1689 by Reverend John Eliot (1604–1690), pastor of the Roxbury Meetinghouse and "Apostle to the Indians." The present school building was erected in 1832, and remodeled by the architect John A. Fox in 1889, when the school was opened to adults who wished to learn metal work, cabinetmaking, arts, and crafts. (Courtesy of William Dillon.)

A Saturday morning sewing class was held at the Eliot School for girls over the age of six. Instructor Beatrice Donoghue, standing second from the right, would show the girls how to embroider after they had mastered plain sewing. (Courtesy of the BPL.)

50

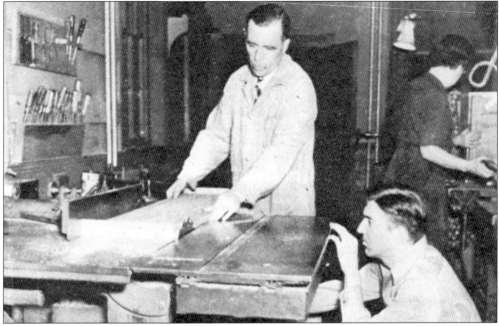

In 1955, instructor Warren E. Bumpus and student William Brown, kneeling, participated in a woodworking course at the Eliot School two evenings a week. (Courtesy of the BPL.)

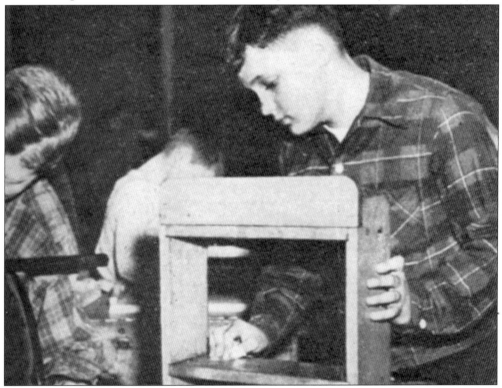

In this picture, Robert Rodday, at the left, is working on a table, while William Connaughton works on a wall shelf during a Saturday morning manual arts class at the Eliot School.

The Academy of Stephen Minot Weld was established in 1827 and became a well-known preparatory school at the corner of Centre and South Streets, opposite the Loring-Greenough House. Weld, for whom Weld Hall at Harvard was named, taught young men at his academy until it was destroyed by fire in 1846. (Courtesy of the BPL.)

The West Roxbury High School, or Eliot High School, was designed by the architectural firm of Cummings and Sears and was built in 1867 on Elm Street for students of West Roxbury. From 1851 to 1874, West Roxbury also included Jamaica Plain and Roslindale. In this photograph are, from left to right: Marion Westcott, Susie Hibbard, and Janet Lord. (Courtesy of the Jamaica Plain Historical Society.)

Members of the Class of 1892 at the Jamaica Plain High School (formerly the West Roxbury High School) pose on the front steps of the school for their class photograph. Above the lintel inscribed, "Eliot High School" are the dates 1689, the year the school was endowed by John Eliot, and 1867, the year the school was built. (Courtesy of the West Roxbury Historical Society.)

Members of the Class of 1907 pose for their class portrait. (Courtesy of the BPL.)

The Jamaica Plain High School was built in 1900 and is an impressive Tudor Revival school. In 1925, an addition was built with an art room, science labs, a lunchroom, and girls' lockers. This school was one of the first in the school system equipped with electric clocks, which were made by the Blodgett Clock Company. (Courtesy of David Rooney.)

Pictured are the 1955 baseball team of Jamaica Plain High School. From left to right are: (front row) Joseph Martin, William Young, John Sylvester, John Ferguson, Robert Reveliotis, and Michael Scipione; (middle row) Murray Hufnagle, Steven Ross, Richard Avakian, John Towsey, Stephen Theodore, and Coach Bond; (back row) William McIntyre, George Hall, Edward Burns, Alfred Brothers, and Norman Dion. (Courtesy of the BPL.)

In this 1941 photograph are the Jamaica Plain High School Cadets, Tenth Regiment. From left to right are: (front row) William Hickey, George Fayad, John Norman, Aloysius MacIntyre, Eugene Kamenides, William De Pasquale, Richard Walsh, and Alexander Marsolini; (middle row) George Berman, Manuel Witt, Frank Catrone, William Bennett, John Smith, Hoffiz Gibran, Robert Hayes, and Robert Higgins; (third row) Edward Horne, Warren Shaw, Charles Fraser, Richard Hunt, Thomas Sarofeen, Charles Pauley, Harold Lowell, and George Anderson. (Courtesy of the BPL.)

Members of the agricultural department at the Jamaica Plain High School in 1959 included, from the left: Robert Antonellis, Jo Ann Butler, Phyllis Burbank, Karen Hicks, C. Willard Bennett, and Mr. Crowley. (Courtesy of the BPL.)

Cheerleaders of the Jamaica Plain High School in 1956 were, from left to right: Barbara Spinney, Catherine Gotovitch, Mary Parlon, Claire Boyce, Lorraine Dustin, Ann Kearns, Ann Lynch, Beatrice Canny, Betty Ann Fetler, Joyce Mutlow, Gwenneth Edwards, Mary Jo McLaughlin, and Marilyn Guiva (kneeling in the center). (Courtesy of the BPL.)

Fore! Members of the girl's golf team in 1945 included, from the left: Carol Krug, Annabel Sampson, Bernice Kohl, Agnes Berghaus, Patricia Regele, Kathleen White, Muriel Stanger, Marguerite Hemmer, Miss Johnson, Barbara Eaton, Nancy O'Hare, Dorothy Scheffler, Marjorie Schwartz, Mary Sorgi, and Florence Blais. (Courtesy of the BPL.)

Participating in Drill Day in 1945 were, from left to right: Mr. James Duffy, Headmaster John Casey, Major Jackson, Lieutenant McDonough, Colonel Smith, unidentified, Lieutenant Waldron, and Lieutenant Frank Famulari. (Courtesy of the BPL.)

Members of the Jamaica Plain High School Cadets in 1956 included, from left to right: (first row) Donald Smith, Gerald Buckley, Robert Carr, and Robert Julio; (middle row) Richard Bavill, Paul Illingworth, Bernard McGonagle, Francis Mazzie, Drum Major Andrew Puleo, David Hartl, Charles McGettrick, John Drinkwater, and their director; (back row) David Rando, Robert Long, Lloyd Weldon, Edward Dowgialo, David McKeen, and Gerald Tousignant. (Courtesy of the BPL.)

The Bowditch School for girls was built in 1892 on Green Street, and was designed by Harrison H. Atwood, Boston city architect.

The Bowditch School was named in memory of Nathaniel Bowditch (1773–1838), a noted astronomer, mathematician, and insurance executive. His book *The Practical Navigator* is still used in the plotting of ships' courses. He served as president of the American Academy of Arts and Sciences from 1829 until his death.

In the Assembly Hall on the third floor of the Bowditch School, the students sit on long benches facing the stage where the headmaster and the teachers sit beneath a marble bust of Nathaniel Bowditch.

Class I in 1893 at the Bowditch School sits at their desks for the photographer. A photograph of the school's facade is on the teacher's desk on the left, and potted plants thrive on shelves mounted before the windows.

Class V at the Bowditch School practice their sewing. Manual arts training was instituted in the Boston public schools by Mary Porter Tileston Hemenway, a member of the Boston School Committee and a philanthropist who personally funded the project for three years. After beginning with plain sewing, students would eventually be taught to sew and even to tailor garments.

Standing in dresses that they had sewn themselves, students of the Bowditch School pose with Master Edward W. Schuerch on the steps of the school.

Cooking classes were part of the curriculum at the Bowditch School. With muslin over-dresses protecting their clothes and mop caps, these students begin their preparations for a lesson on baking.

A student bends down in front of the stove to place her pan filled with batter in the cast iron stove. These cooking lessons allowed students who weren't contemplating college a means of earning a living after graduation.

The office of Master Edward W. Schuerch of the Bowditch School had a roll-top oak desk and an entire wall lined with overflowing bookcases.

The janitor at the Bowditch School had a comfortable and cozy room in the basement. With an upholstered sofa, a wicker lounge chair, and geraniums on a ledge, the room seemed a pleasant place where he could relax between catastrophes.

A young student stands in front of the "Westchester Portable" School on Westchester Road, off Centre Street in Jamaica Plain. (Courtesy of the Jamaica Plain Historical Society.)

Old Agassiz School

The Old Agassiz School, located on Burroughs Street, was a three-story brick schoolhouse with a bracketed pediment. This was the old Central School of West Roxbury, built in 1849. (Courtesy of David Rooney.)

The Agassiz School was named in honor of Louis Agassiz (1807–1873), who was professor of zoology at Harvard from 1848 to 1873. A native of Switzerland, he was a naturalist who became one of the most knowledgeable professors in his field. His wife, Ida Higginson Agassiz, was the founder of Radcliffe College.

The second Agassiz School, photographed in 1933, is located at the corner of Burroughs and Brewer Streets. (Courtesy of David Rooney.)

The Francis Parkman School, a
Romanesque Revival schoolhouse, was
built on Walk Hill Street in Forest Hills
by the architectural firm of Perkins and
Beeton in 1899. (Courtesy of the West
Roxbury Historical Society.)

The Parkman School was named for
Francis Parkman (1823–1893), a noted
historian who lived near Jamaica Pond in
the mid-nineteenth century. He is best
known for his history course of the Anglo-
French conflict in North America.

The Wyman School was a small Romanesque Revival schoolhouse on Wyman Street, and was built in 1892. (Courtesy of David Rooney.)

The Mary E. Curley School was built in 1931 and was named for the wife of Boston Mayor James Michael Curley. Built on the corner of Centre Street and Pershing Road, the school was a lively art deco structure designed by the architectural firm of McLaughlin and Burr. (Courtesy of David Rooney.)

Five
Arnold Arboretum and Forest Hills Cemetery

A group of visitors to the Arnold Arboretum at the turn of the century passes by a profuse display of mountain laurel. In spring, summer, and fall, something was in bloom at the arboretum. During the winter the evergreens proved impressive sentinels along the hills.

James Arnold, a wealthy New Bedford merchant, bequeathed a large sum of money to Harvard College. The money was used to establish the Arnold Arboretum in 1872, on the former estate of Benjamin Bussey. Arnold's home, now the Waumsutta Club on County Street, was the site of the spectacular garden known as "Arnold's Garden."

The Bussey Institute was named in memory of Benjamin Bussey (1757–1842), who bequeathed his estate for the benefit of Harvard College. His estate was used to establish the Bussey Institute and to further endow the Law School and Divinity School at Harvard.

Charles Sprague Sargent, standing on the right, was appointed in 1873 as the first director of the Arnold Arboretum. He was of the chair of arboriculture at Harvard and author of *The Sylva of North America*. Seated to the left of Sargent is his cousin John Singer Sargent, the noted painter.

A crew of workers prepares the driveway in front of the museum at the Arnold Arboretum at the turn of the century. (Courtesy of the BPL.)

A series of circuitous roads laid out through the Arnold Arboretum allowed visitors to walk through the garden or to drive their carriage along the roads at a slow pace.

A woman walks along a path bordered by lilac bushes. "Lilac Sunday" is one of the more popular, as well as fragrant, Sundays at the Arnold Arboretum.

A young girl looks at native grape vines that have been trained on a trellis. In the foreground is *vitis bicolor*.

Looking toward Boston from the top of Bussey Hill, the view is absolutely stupendous. In this turn-of-the-century picture, one can see the museum (now the Hunnewell Building). Through the trees is a view of Jamaica Plain.

The museum at the Arnold Arboretum is known as the Hunnewell Building, in honor of Horatio Hollis Hunnewell, who donated the building in 1892 and supported the arboretum after its founding. The first floor was originally the dendrological museum and the second floor the library.

A sure sign of spring after a long cold winter is the blossoming of cherry trees. Here, across a mirrored pond, the first cherry trees bloom and signal the beginning of three seasons of beautiful color.

The entrance to Forest Hills Cemetery, erected in 1865, is an impressive Gothic gate of Roxbury puddingstone and Caledonia freestone. Henry A.S. Dearborn (1783–1851), a mayor of Roxbury and president of the Massachusetts Horticultural Society, created Forest Hills from the Joel Seaverns Farm as an arboretum cemetery. He wanted the cemetery to be a combination of burial lots, monuments, and natural landscape so that it would be a place to not only visit the dead but to mourn them more naturally. On the right is Forsyth Chapel. (Courtesy of William Dillon.)

An impressive Receiving Tomb was erected at Forest Hills in 1870, with a Gothic portico of white Concord granite and a floor paved with black and white marble tiles. A garden with flower beds surround a cast-iron fountain in the foreground.

Spectacular displays, such as this topiary crown and the surrounding jewel-like pattern of multi-colored flowers, were planted by the groundskeepers at Forest Hills in the late nineteenth century. These bedding displays must have taken many hours to plan and plant as well as to tend, and were an impressive aspect of arboretum cemeteries.

William J. Hargraves was appointed superintendent of Forest Hills in 1896, after having cared for the Jamaica Plain estate of J. Ingersoll Bowditch. A knowledgeable horticulturist, it was said of Hargraves that he was "eminently fitted for the position of superintendent" at Forest Hills Cemetery. (Courtesy of the West Roxbury Historical Society.)

Lake Hibiscus is in the center of Forest Hills Cemetery and is reached by winding paths that lead to this pleasant place to contemplate nature. Today, swans, named Gracie and Fred, and ducks enjoy both the summer months at the lake and the food that is offered to them by visitors.

The Soldiers Monument at Forest Hills Cemetery, sculpted by Martin Milmore (1844–1883), is a bronze statue of a volunteer soldier. It was erected in 1867 by the City of Roxbury to commemorate the heroism of soldiers who served in the Civil War. After Roxbury was annexed to Boston in 1868, Forest Hills Cemetery became a private corporation. (Courtesy of William F. Clark.)

The memorial at Forest Hills to George Robert White (1847–1922) is an impressive bronze angel sculpted by Daniel Chester French. White left his fortune "for creating works of public utility and beauty for the use and enjoyment of the inhabitants of the City of Boston"; the income is still used to support health centers throughout the city neighborhoods.

The Cremator at Forest Hills Cemetery was the first in the United States. There are two chapels, the Lucy Stone and William J. Pitman Chapels. Lucy Stone (1818–1893) was the first Massachusetts woman to graduate from college (Oberlin), the first Massachusetts woman editor (*The Woman's Journal*), the first person to be cremated in the United States (at the Forest Hills Crematorium), and is believed to be the first woman to retain her maiden name after her marriage.

Six

Jamaica Pond

A group of men enjoy a game of curling on Jamaica Pond at the turn of the century. A Scottish game using rounded, flat-bottomed granite stones that are pushed by a straw broom toward a mark, curling was quite a popular sport, once the pond froze solid. (Courtesy of the BPL.)

Skating on Jamaica Pond was a popular winter activity in the nineteenth century. Here, skaters twirl about the frozen pond alone and in groups. Notice the houses built along the shore of the pond. The houses were later demolished, after the land was purchased by the City of Boston for the Olmstead-designed park. (Courtesy of the BPL.)

In an 1858 painting by H.R. Hunt, aptly titled *Skating on Jamaica Pond*, these skaters seem to be enjoying an afternoon spin, even though a few of the skaters have taken a tumble. In 1855, Elizabeth Mason Cabot made reference in her diary to a "new amusement that has arisen on the Boston horizon: skating."

Shares. **$**

JAMAICA POND AQUEDUCT COMPANY.

Incorp'd May 8, 1857.   Shares, $100 Each.

BE IT KNOWN, *That*   *is*

Proprietor of   *Shares in the Capital Stock of the*

Jamaica Pond Aqueduct Corporation,

the Assessment on said Shares having been paid in full. Said Shares
are Transferable at the office of the President of
said Corporation.
Witness the signatures of the President and Treasurer of the said

Corporation,   *18*

President,

Treasurer.

The Jamaica Pond Aqueduct Company was incorporated in 1857 to provide fresh water to the residents of Jamaica Plain. The pond was a "kettle hole" created by the Ice Age glaciers that carved it out of the earth. The water originally came from the melting ice. Later, water was taken from the underground springs that had opened when the kettle was created.

Jamaica Pond had been used for ice harvesting since the eighteenth century. By the mid-nineteenth century, icehouses were built along the shoreline to house the ice prior to shipment. Men stand with horse-drawn sleds that were used to convey the cut ice to the icehouses. (Courtesy of the BPL.)

The ice on Jamaica Pond is being scored by horse-drawn ice ploughs. Once scored, the plough would again cut the ice at a ninety degree angle to form a block of ice that was easier to handle. The long, low building in the distance is an icehouse. (Courtesy of the BPL.)

The ice has been cut into squares by the horse-drawn ploughs and is ready for "ice harvesting." Once put on a horse-drawn sled, the ice would be brought to the shed (seen in the foreground). There the ice blocks were hoisted into the icehouse by a conveyor belt, seen on the left. Once stored, the ice was usually covered in sawdust and was later shipped throughout the world. (Courtesy of the BPL.)

During the mid-nineteenth century, pedimented wood icehouses lined the shore of Jamaica Pond. However, as early as the 1880s, the pond was being used more for recreation than for ice harvesting, as the rowboats in the foreground connote. (Courtesy of the West Roxbury Historical Society.)

Local delivery of ice by the Jamaica Pond Ice Company was delivered to residences for use in iceboxes, which were wood chests lined with zinc that allowed food to stay fresh for a day or two. Here two delivery men using ice tongs hold blocks of ice that had been cut to the proper size for the new iceboxes. If the block proved too large, it could be reduced in size with an ice pick. (Courtesy of the BPL.)

By the turn of the century, the icehouses had been demolished. The area surrounding Jamaica Pond had been embellished with trees and shrubs by Frederick Law Olmstead between 1878 and 1895 as a part of Boston's "Emerald Necklace."

Looking down a path that leads to Jamaica Pond, one can readily see how attractive the area was for walking during the warm summer months. (Courtesy of the BPL.)

With park benches, mature shade trees, and a placid Jamaica Pond, the pleasures of strolling along the pond have been enjoyed for many generations.

By 1912, the City of Boston had built a boathouse (on the left), a landing, and a shelter of a Tudor wattle and daub design by Dorchester architect William Downer Austin. A continuous wooden bench encircles the lawn and allows for a panoramic view of Jamaica Pond.

Strollers walk along Jamaica Pond about 1910, as canoeists traverse the pond.

"The Cove" at Jamaica Pond was a popular place for visiting by courting couples. A woman holds a parasol to shield her from the sun as her beau admires the view.

Girls feed the swans that glided along Jamaica Pond.

A flock of swans swims toward the edge of Jamaica Pond at the turn of the century.

Swans glide and bask in the sun at Jamaica Pond. Notice the life preserver mounted to a pole for swimmers or over-zealous swan feeders.

An ice-skating race was held on Jamaica Pond in 1923 to the delighted roars of the spectators. (Courtesy of the BPL.)

Seven

A Medley of Community Services

An instructor at the Children's Museum discusses mounted birds to a group of boys, or "Sons of Nature," at the old museum. Taxidermists would mount animals that could be studied in the museum and displayed in cabinets, such as in the background. (Courtesy of the BPL.)

A group of students and their teachers pose on the front porch of Pinebank, which had been loaned by the Boston Park Department to the Children's Museum. After the Perkins family sold Pinebank to the City of Boston in 1891, the building was used as office headquarters for the Park Department until 1913, when the Children's Museum took possession. (Courtesy of the BPL.)

A group of boys from the geology class at the Children's Museum in 1915 are ready for a field trip, complete with hammers. Trips were led by Robert W. Sayles, whose talks on geology inspired the boys for their Saturday morning geological surveys. (Courtesy of the West Roxbury Historical Society.)

A group of children look at examples of birds that have been mounted by taxidermists and displayed in the former drawing room of Pinebank. (Courtesy of the BPL.)

In 1936, through the generosity of the Godfrey M. Hymans Fund, Inc., the Children's Museum moved to the former Morse-Mitton House, at the corner of Burroughs Street and the Jamaicaway. An impressive twenty-eight-room Colonial Revival mansion, it was built at the turn of the century and served as the museum until it moved in 1979 to its present location in Boston. (Courtesy of the BPL.)

A group of children study some of the ever-changing exhibits at the Children's Museum. The exhibits broadened their knowledge and stimulated their minds.

On Saturday mornings at the Children's Museum, members of the Hobby Club met in the library.

The Grand Army of the Republic, No. 200, a group of Civil War veterans, met in the former West Roxbury town hall on Thomas Street. The building served the town from 1851 until 1868, when Curtis Hall was built through the generosity of Nelson Curtis. (Courtesy of the BPL.)

A young girl sits on the stone wall surrounding the property of the Jamaica Club. Built in 1889 at the corner of Elm and Green Streets, the club was a rambling series of rooms where club members could play billiards, enjoy card games, and socialize. The elm on the left was often referred to as the "Liberty Elm" and was one of the largest trees in the vicinity of Boston.

Eliot Hall has been the home of the Footlight Club since 1878, when a drawing room comedy, *A Scrap of Paper*, was performed by members of the club. Organized on January 4, 1877, the premise of the Footlight Club was to promote friendly and social intercourse and furnish pleasant useful entertainment by aid of drama. (Courtesy of the West Roxbury Historical Society.)

Grace Hiler was a member of the Jamaica Plain Tuesday Club. She was photographed in London as a bridesmaid for a wedding. A faithful and active member of the club, she bequeathed a large sum of money to further its goals. (Courtesy of the BPL.)

A program cover for a performance of the Footlight Club in Jamaica Plain had this rendition of a cavalier. (Courtesy of the BPL.)

This ticket granted one admission to the 100th performance of the Footlight Club at Eliot Hall on May 4, 1906. (Courtesy of the BPL.)

The fiftieth anniversary of the Geschichte Des Boylston Schul-Verein was celebrated in 1924. Jamaica Plain and Roxbury had large numbers of German immigrants who worked in the breweries along the Stony Brook and attended these enjoyable social events. (Courtesy of the BPL.)

The Italian Home for Children is at the corner of Centre Street and Westchester Road. Incorporated in 1919, it offered care for children whose parents were unable to support them. (Courtesy of the West Roxbury Historical Society.)

The Massachusetts Society for the Prevention of Cruelty to Animals (MSPCA) was originally in this building in the Fenway, but moved to the corner of South Huntington Avenue and Perkins Street in Jamaica Plain. The first newspaper concerning the care of animals, *Our Dumb Animals*, was started in 1868.

George T. Angell (1823–1909) founded the Massachusetts Society for the Prevention of Cruelty to Animals (MSPCA) and the American Humane Education Society.

At the turn of the century, the Perkins Institution for the Blind had a branch in Jamaica Plain, at the corner of Day and Perkins Streets. Commonly referred to as the "Kindergarten for the Blind," the school was founded in 1887 to prepare blind children under the age of nine for a lifetime of self-respect and to be self-supporting members of society. The buildings were segregated for boys and girls.

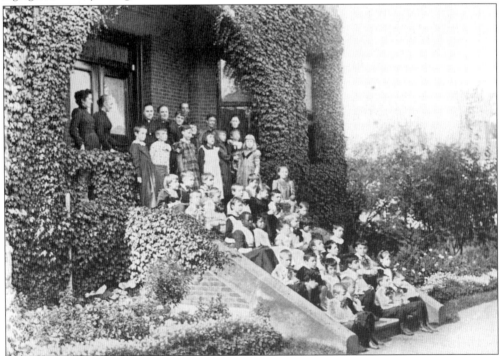

Students of the "Kindergarten for the Blind" pose on the stairs to the Perkins Institution in Jamaica Plain in 1903. Dedicated in 1887, the school was an outgrowth of the Perkins Institution for the Blind in South Boston, founded by Samuel Gridley Howe and continued by his son-in-law, Michael Anagos.

Miss Roeske, second from the left in the rear row, taught students in her music appreciation class to play musical instruments. The students often gave informal concerts for the other students and their visitors.

Every morning, children at the kindergarten would gather in a circle for a morning talk.

Children would be accepted at the "Kindergarten for the Blind" at the age of five. Here, students sit at tables while supervised by their teacher, and they participate in the "lesson in the first gift."

The kindergarten was not all work. Often games would be played, such as this one with a student in the center who has a belt with attached leads that each of the students hold.

Mary Faulkner (1859–1896) was the daughter of Dr. George Faulkner, for whom the Faulkner Hospital in Jamaica Plain was named. (Courtesy of the BPL.)

In 1924, Faulkner Hospital was built on Centre Street, at the corner of Allandale Street. The hospital building can be glimpsed through the dense wood of trees.

Dr. George Faulkner was a beloved physician who practiced medicine in West Roxbury, Roslindale, and West Roxbury in the nineteenth century.

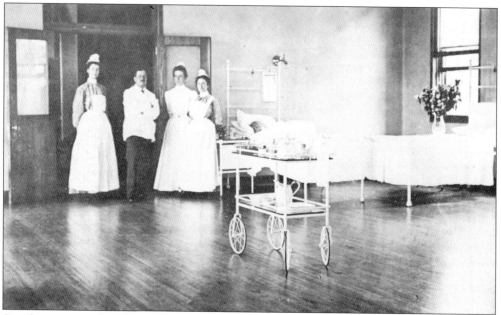

Standing in a ward at the Faulkner Hospital at the turn of the century are, from left to right: Nurse Clara Penquilly, Dr. J.H.S. Leard, Nurse Gamage, and Nurse Anna Berquod. (Courtesy of the BPL.)

The Class of 1905 from the Faulkner Hospital School of Nursing pose for their graduation photograph. (Courtesy of the BPL.)

A new building was built for the Faulkner Hospital facing Centre Street. (Courtesy of the West Roxbury Historical Society.)

The Veterans Administration Hospital was built at the corner of South Huntington Avenue and Heath Street. On the left can be seen the New England Baptist Hospital on Parker Hill.

The Lemuel Shattuck Hospital on Morton Street, adjacent to Franklin Park at Forest Hills, was named for Lemuel Shattuck, a member of the Massachusetts House of Representatives and a founder of the New England Historic and Genealogical Society in 1845. This family portrait, painted by Bass Otis, shows Shattuck on the left with his wife and many daughters. (Courtesy of the BPL.)

The Adams Nervine Hospital was founded in 1880 by sugar merchant Seth Adams and was located at 990 Centre Street in the J. Gardiner Weld House. Weld had died before he could occupy it. The Weld House served not only as doctors' offices but patients' rooms, as one of the concepts of the Adams Nervine was to treat patients with nervous disorders in a home-like setting. The hospital merged with Faulkner Hospital in 1975, and the house is now part of the Adams-Arboretum condominium complex. (Courtesy of the Jamaica Plain Historical Society.)

The Emerson Hospital was at 118 Forest Hills Street in the former A. Davis Weld House. Founded in 1904, the Emerson Hospital dealt with medical, surgical, and maternity cases in a private home setting rather than an institutional one.

Children stand on the stairs of the Sedgwick Street Branch of the Boston Public Library in Jamaica Plain about 1928. The branch library began in 1876 when a book delivery took place in Curtis Hall. By 1909, this building was started and has been an active branch ever since. (Courtesy of the West Roxbury Historical Society.)

At the Main Charging Desk, one could check out books with the help of an obliging librarian, if you were in good standing. (Courtesy of the West Roxbury Historical Society.)

A librarian reads to young patrons in the Children's Room of the library in 1928. Notice the massive fireplace and mantle behind the remarkably well-behaved children. (Courtesy of the West Roxbury Historical Society.)

Patrons read at a library table in the Adult Reading Room in 1928. (Courtesy of the West Roxbury Historical Society.)

Many of the activities held at the library attracted numerous children. Here, children decorate Easter eggs in 1967. Some of the artists have rollers in their hair for a perfect coiffure on Easter Sunday. (Courtesy of the BPL.)

At a Christmas Open House at the library in 1966, Mrs. John F. Collins, the wife of Boston's mayor who served from 1960 to 1966, pours tea. From right to left are: Right Reverend Edward G. Murray, Geraldine M. Altman (branch librarian), Mrs. Christopher Iannella, and Raymond McCulloch (president of the Friends of the Jamaica Plain Branch Library). (Courtesy of the BPL.)

Eight
A Streetcar Suburb

Centre Street in the mid-1880s had become a bustling commercial district. On the right is White's Block, which featured Jamaica Hardware and Plumbing, Margot the Florist, and the real estate office of Robert T. Fowler. A horse-drawn streetcar travels south towards Burroughs Street. (Courtesy of the West Roxbury Historical Society.)

The corner of Centre and Burroughs Streets had the Burroughs Block, an impressive panel brick and brownstone commercial building built in 1888 and designed by George A. Cahill (on the left) and Sweatt & Company Pharmacists (on the right). A fruit-filled cart stands in front of Keazer's Store. (Courtesy of William Dillon.)

A streetcar travels north on Centre Street in 1912. On the right is the tower of the Burrough's Building, and two men are walking towards Keazer's Fruit Store. On the left is White's Block. (Courtesy of the Jamaica Plain Historical Society.)

The Burroughs Block, located at the corner of Centre and Burroughs Streets, was designed by George A. Cahill. C.B. Rogers & Company Pharmacists were located on the first floor; Charles B. Rogers had established his pharmacy in 1867. (Courtesy of the Jamaica Plain Historical Society.)

The Woolsey Block in 1895 was an impressive four-story commercial block with Nelson's Grocery Store, the Jamaica Plain News Depot, and the West Roxbury Co-operative Bank. On the left, a carriage waits outside the Jamaica Plain train station. (Courtesy of William Dillon.)

Eugene Noble Foss (1858–1939) was governor of Massachusetts from 1911 to 1913. His home in Jamaica Plain, which had been built in 1890 by his father-in-law at 11 Revere Street on Sumner Hill, is now listed on the National Register of Historic Places. Foss was associated with B.F. Sturtevant Company, a metal products and blower manufactory, which was founded by his father-in-law, Benjamin Franklin Sturtevant (1833–1890).

Sigourney Street runs from Walnut Avenue to Glen Road, along the western border of Franklin Park. Laid out with impressive houses between 1875 and the turn of the century, it was once part of the estate of Samuel Goodrich, who was known as "Peter Parley." (Courtesy of the BPL.)

Andrew J. Peters (1872–1938) was mayor of Boston from 1918 to 1921, and lived in the old Weld House on South Street in Forest Hills. A one-time state senator, it was said of him that he was "active and faithful in the discharge of his duties and has interested himself in measures that were at once practical and wholesome."

Designed by William Ralph Emerson (1833–1917), the "father of Shingle Style" architecture, for J. Greenough in 1880, this house epitomizes Emerson's architectural talent in combining different shingling, projecting bays, Queen Anne chimneys, and fanciful wood turnings. Greenough had inherited the land on Sumner Hill from his family.

Bailey Little Page (1850–1912) was a land developer who lived at 2 Alveston Street on Sumner Hill. By the turn of the century, Page owned and controlled a large amount of real estate in Jamaica Plain.

Designed by William Ralph Emerson, this house on Greenough Street on Sumner Hill combined both the Shingle Style and Colonial Revival forms of architecture.

Elm Street runs from Roanoke Street to Sedgwick Street on Sumner Hill. Here, a car nears Saint John's Episcopal Church, which can be seen through the trees.

Westerly Street runs from Centre Street to Sunnyside Street in the Hyde Square section of Jamaica Plain. It was named for "Westerly", the area which became West Roxbury in 1851.

An apartment block was built by Benjamin Fox between 1905 and 1908 on Centre Street, between Lakeville and Beaufort Roads. The block was built for Ella C. Adams, whose estate abutted the development, and now it is the site of the Rogerson House. Built of brick and rough-hewn brownstone, these apartments (Lakeville Terrace and Beaufort Terrace) epitomize the "Streetcar Suburb" aspect of Jamaica Plain.

Nine

Forest Hills

The Toll Gate Inn was a popular pub on Walk Hill Street in Forest Hills. Washington Street, which was laid out in 1805 from downtown Boston to Providence, Rhode Island, was originally a toll road, and the toll booth was at Forest Hills. Two young boys stand on the steps to this fanciful Shingle Style pub in 1900. (Courtesy of David Rooney.)

The Morton Block, which was built in 1881 at the corner of Hyde Park Avenue and Washington Street in Forest Hills, was a large grocery store with apartments on the second and third floors. (Courtesy of the West Roxbury Historical Society.)

Michael S. Morton was a successful grocer in Jamaica Plain and an active member of the Jamaica Plain Citizens Association. He lived at 75 Morton Street in Jamaica Plain. (Courtesy of the West Roxbury Historical Society.)

The Minton Block was a three-story commercial block in Forest Hills. Built by Thomas Minton, he was "known as a man who has been a great factor in the development of this section."

Thomas F. Minton was a successful contractor and land developer who laid out Skinner Hill in Roslindale, the area of "Forest Garden" (Peter Parley Road, Park Lane, etc.), and the Weld Estate (Tower, Woodlawn, and Weld Hill Streets) in Jamaica Plain. He later developed the Parker Estate and laid out Brookside Avenue, Cable, Marmion, and Minton Streets. (Courtesy of the West Roxbury Historical Society.)

Looking south on Hyde Park Avenue at Forest Hills, the Minton Block is on the left and the Morton Block on the right. (Courtesy of David Rooney.)

Three horses drink from a water trough in the center of Forest Hills at the turn of the century. Streetcars are parked near a stop of the Boston and Providence Railroad. (Courtesy of the Roslindale Historical Society.)

Forest Hills Square is the junction of Washington, Morton, South, and Walk Hill Streets, and Hyde Park Avenue. In this picture, streetcars approach the square from the south.

The construction of the Elevated Railway in Forest Hills caused disruption and chaos for almost three years. On the left is the Boston and Providence Railroad. The approach of the elevated railway can be seen on Washington Street in the distance. (Courtesy of David Rooney.)

The Forest Hills Station became the terminus for the Boston Elevated Railway in 1909. Designed by the architect Edmund March Wheelwright (1854–1912), the station was built of reinforced concrete with copper embellishments.

The Forest Hills Station, in this 1940 photograph, was a major terminus for passengers continuing on to Roslindale, West Roxbury, Dedham, and beyond. A parking lot for commuters' cars was provided for ease of transportation via the "El." (Courtesy of the West Roxbury Historical Society.)

Ten
Modes of
Transportation

A horse-drawn streetcar stops in 1880, in front of the car barn of the Metropolitan Street Railway, at the corner of South and Jamaica Streets. (Courtesy of the BPL.)

The Jamaica Plain depot at Green Street, on the New Haven Railroad line, brought commuters to town prior to the Civil War. The area developed due to the proximity of the railroad and the accessibility to Boston, and after the tracks were elevated to eliminate the grade crossing.

Looking north on Centre Street from Burroughs Street, a horse-drawn streetcar passes a rapidly changing street scene. Centre Street was once a residential street, but by the 1870s, it was becoming increasingly more commercial. (Courtesy of the BPL.)

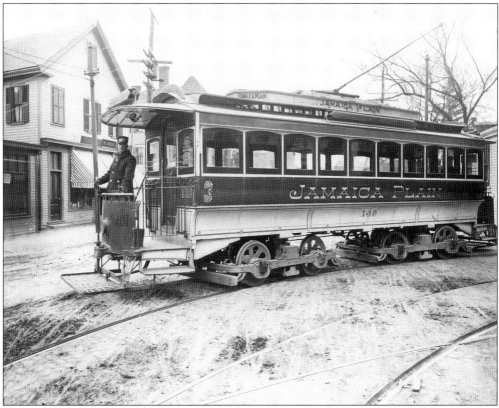

Streetcar 149 stops outside the Jamaica Plain car house in 1898. These electrically powered streetcars replaced the ever faithful horses of the street railways. (Courtesy of David Rooney.)

Passengers enter a streetcar on Centre Street about 1900 to go to "town."

Streetcars that serviced Jamaica Plain along South Huntington Avenue and terminated at Forest Hills Station on the Boston Elevated Railway were often paired, due to the large number of passengers. (Courtesy of David Rooney.)

The interior of Car 5816 was photographed in 1935. The wood-slatted seats looked uncomfortable, and a wood-ribbed floor caught water from umbrellas and raincoats. (Courtesy of David Rooney.)

A streetcar heads north on Centre Street in 1912. (Courtesy of the BPL.)

A streetcar passes workmen excavating at the junction of South Huntington Avenue and Centre Street in 1930. Notice the crenelated tower on the three-decker at the corner of Centre and Boylston Streets. (Courtesy of David Rooney.)

A two-car train of all-electric PCC cars travels south on Centre Street in the early 1960s. (Courtesy of the BPL.)

By 1906, the Elevated Railway had reached the area of Green and Washington Streets. The "El" was extended from Dudley Street in Roxbury to Forest Hill in 1909. The stations along Washington Street were Egleston Square Station, added in 1909, and Green Street Station, added in 1912. The Elevated Railway cast a dark shadow along Washington Street for seventy years, until it was demolished in the mid-1970s. (Courtesy of David Rooney.)

Looking southwest on Washington Street from Green Street, the excavations for the construction of the Elevated Railway can be seen in this photograph from 1906. (Courtesy of David Rooney.)

The trustees for the Boston Elevated Railway in 1929 were, from left to right: Edward E. Whiting, George B. Johnson, Henry I. Harriman (chairman), Charles H. Cole, and Ernest A. Johnson.

127

Acknowledgments

I would like to thank the following for their assistance in researching this book on Jamaica Plain, Massachusetts, and their continued support and interest:

Daniel J. Ahlin, Anthony Bognanno, Paul and Helen Graham Buchanan, Jamie Carter, William F. Clark, Marian Connor, Martha Tyer Curtis, the late Nelson Curtis Jr., Reverend Elizabeth Curtiss, Dexter, William Dillon, the Faulkner Hospital, Forest Hills Cemetery, Edward W. Gordon, Richard and Nancy Foss Heath, the Jamaica Plain Historical Society, David and Judith Kunze, James Z. Kyprianos, Leslie C. Loke, Robert J. MacMillan, M.D., John Franklin May, the late Dagmar Pierce Merna, Robert Murphy, David Nathan, New England Baptist Hospital, Marilyn Oberle, Stephen and Susan Paine, Reverend Michael Parise, David Rooney, the Roslindale Historical Society, Dennis Ryan, Anthony and Mary Mitchell Sammarco, Rosemary Sammarco, the Lemuel Shattuck Hospital, Stanley Slotnick, Sandra Storey of Gazette Publications, Anne and George Thompson, William and Martha Varrell, the West Roxbury Historical Society, Virginia White, Elizabeth Shaw Williams, Susan Williams, Alice Roberts (branch librarian), and the staff of the Jamaica Plain Branch of the Boston Public Library.